BATTLE OF NEW ORLEANS

LECTOR HOUSE PUBLIC DOMAIN WORKS

BATTLE OF NEW ORLEANS

REAU ESTES FOLK

ISBN: 978-93-90294-67-1

Published: -

© 2020
LECTOR HOUSE LLP

LECTOR HOUSE

LECTOR HOUSE LLP
E-MAIL: lectorpublishing@gmail.com

BATTLE OF NEW ORLEANS

ITS REAL MEANING

EXPOSURE OF UNTRUTH BEING TAUGHT YOUNG AMERICA

Concerning the Second Most Important Military Event in the Life of the Republic.

BY

REAU E. FOLK,

*Chairman Tennessee Commission of Research as to the True Value of
the Victory at New Orleans.*

DEDICATION

This Volume Is Dedicated To:

The State of Tennessee, which authorized the Investigation;

The Ladies' Hermitage Association, charged with primary duty of preserving the home of Andrew Jackson, whose military genius, courage, and patriotism saved the nation in the second War of Independence;

The Descendants of the Soldiers who fought at New Orleans, whose memory should always be cherished; and

The noble band of School Teachers everywhere, whose high impulse is to impart the truth.

REAU E. FOLK.

Nashville, Tenn.

CONTENTS

COMMISSION REPORT

Below is given report to the Governor of Tennessee by the author of this volume as chairman of the authorized Tennessee Committee of Research. Attached are letters of concurrence from two of his associate members. The remaining member is out of the country. Documents have been sent to him, but at the time of this printing sufficient time has not elapsed to hear from him. In a later edition his comments will be given.

NASHVILLE, TENNESSEE
To His Excellency, The Honorable Hill McAllister,
Governor of Tennessee.

Sir:

The General Assembly of Tennessee of 1927 adopted the following joint resolution:

WHEREAS, the Battle of New Orleans, fought on January 8, 1815, is one of the outstanding military events of American History; and,

WHEREAS, the memory of the great American victory achieved there, is especially cherished by Tennesseans because of Andrew Jackson, and the other Tennesseans who therein immortalized themselves; and,

WHEREAS, school histories, adopted for and taught in our schools, convey the impression that the battle was a needless one in that it occurred fifteen days after the Treaty of Peace had been signed at Ghent, Belgium, by the Commissioners representing the United States and England; and,

WHEREAS, serious criticism is made that such textbooks present an erroneous appraisement of the value of the battle, by omitting the reference to an essential fact, to-wit: that England did not construe the Peace Treaty of Ghent as applicable to Louisiana, for the reason that she held as invalid the title of the United States to that Domain, conveyed by Napoleon Bonaparte in 1803; and,

WHEREAS, it is of prime importance that our school children should receive every essential truth from historical textbooks, and especially those textbooks placed in the hands of Tennessee students should portray in its true significance the Battle of New Orleans in which the ancestors of so many were engaged; now,

THEREFORE, be it resolved by the Senate, the House of Representatives concurring, that the Governor be, and is hereby empowered and authorized, to appoint five, or in discretion seven, persons of known historical knowledge and research, who shall constitute a Commission, charged with the duty of carefully examining the authorities, touching the true value of the Battle of New Orleans, fought January 8, 1815; and,

Said Commission shall incorporate its conclusions and recommendations in a report to the Governor who shall transmit the same to the Legislature.

Under the above resolution the following were appointed: Reau E. Folk, Chairman; John Trotwood Moore; John H. DeWitt; Claude G. Bowers; John S. Kendall.

The chairman, by reason of partial business retirement, has been able to devote himself assiduously to the research work involved. The result of his research, compiled into a small volume, accompanies this report.

At the outset the writer wishes to say he has had no opportunity for conference with the full Commission, but has had the benefit of consultation with Messrs. Moore and DeWitt, both of whom were very co-operative. The first named, the late John Trotwood Moore, State Historian, condensed his conclusion into a sentence, which is here given because he is no longer with us to speak for himself. He said: "The Battle of New Orleans saved the Louisiana Purchase, or another war with England." Judge John H. DeWitt, President of the Tennessee Historical Society, has given much valuable and sympathetic aid.

The small volume herewith submitted gives exact quotations concerning the Battle of New Orleans from all histories under adoption as textbooks for the public schools of Tennessee. All of these present the same viewpoint, to-wit: that the battle was an unnecessary one; that it was fought after peace had been made. These researches show conclusively that all these books are in error. The battle was NOT fought after peace.

These researches have uncovered a startling, astounding fact—startling and astounding because that fact has been consistently ignored or overlooked by historians. That fact appears in the wording of the Ghent Treaty itself, which says in plain language that peace shall be effective when the treaty shall have been ratified by both sides! It was ratified by the United States February 17, 1815, forty days after the Battle of New Orleans!

Hence it must be patent to all that the statement, that the battle occurred after peace made so persistently by historians, is an obvious untruth, based on false assumption of fact. The wording of the treaty, appearing in the volume herewith, has been verified from the treaty itself on file in the State Department at Washington.

If the issue of the battle had been different, it is a matter for fair speculation as to whether or not the treaty would have been ratified by the United States. The Administration would have been torn between the ominous threats of the northeastern states on the one hand, and on the other by British occupancy of the vast territory west of the Mississippi River, with civil government set up. Happily this grave situation was averted by the great victory, news of which reached Washington ten days before the treaty.

In the volume herewith there is presented well authenticated evidence leading to the irresistable deduction that it was England's purpose after capturing to retain the great Louisiana Domain, on the ground of the invalidity of the U. S. title acquired from Napoleon in 1803. Among other indications of England's attitude there are exhibited copies of records during the negotiations at Ghent taken from the archives of the State Department at Washington.

The chairman, as the compiler of the volume referred to, hopes it will be carefully read by all interested in truth of history, not only in Tennessee, but in the nation.

The writer, in obedience to the Legislative resolution under which he was appointed, herewith asks leave to report as his findings as to the true value of the Battle of New Orleans the following:

1st: It did not occur after peace as erroneously is stated by school and other histories; it occurred during a state of war between the United States and England;

2nd: It was a necessary battle, made so by the aggressions of England; in addition to its national necessity, it was as necessary as would be the defense by a citizen of his home and family from marauders;

3rd: It was a major military event in the life of the Republic, second only to Yorktown;

4th: It saved the Louisiana Purchase, or prolongation of existing war, or another war with England; or acquiescense in the Mississippi River as our western boundary;

5th: It established wholesome respect of U. S. sovereignty by Great Britain, marking the last armed conflict between these two powers, between which a solid peace has existed ever since;

6th: It created profound impression throughout the world, with consequent greater respect and security of the Republic among her sister nations;

7th: It restored national self respect, then at its lowest ebb.

In submitting the result of this research the writer earnestly recommends to the Governor and the General Assembly that proper and decisive steps be taken to the end that our school children may be taught the truth as to the value of the great victory in which Tennesseans of another age played a leading part, and which contributed so much to the destinies of the nation.

Respectfully,
REAU E. FOLK,
Chairman, Authorized Commission of Research as to Value of Battle of New Orleans.

December 12, 1934.

My Dear Mr. Folk:

I have carefully read and considered the report which you, as Chairman of the Commission appointed in 1927 to examine the authorities as to the true value of the Battle of New Orleans, are about to make to the Governor of Tennessee. Hitherto I have had the privilege of conferring with you from time to time concerning the important historical question involved in the investigation.

I have also read carefully the treatise prepared by you and which accompanies your report to the Governor. It shows very thorough and judicious investigation, and in my opinion very sound conclusions.

I fully concur with you in the conclusions stated in your report, as well as the reasons therefor which you have therein set forth in lucid statement.

I do trust that this valuable work which you have done will be properly appreciated, and that the errors which have so persistently appeared in the histories, particularly the school histories, will be duly corrected, so that the fallacy that the Battle of New Orleans was a useless battle and fought after the treaty of peace, will no longer be accepted by anybody, and that truth will be known by all.

Yours very truly,
JOHN H. DEWITT.
D-R

Tulane University,
New Orleans, La.,
December 22, 1934.

My Dear Mr. Folk:

I have read with attention your excellent report on the Battle of New Orleans, to be submitted to the Governor of Tennessee, in conjunction with the report of our commission on the subject. I have ventured to indicate by question marks in two or three places phrases or statements which I think could be changed to advantage. These, however, are merely questions of verbiage, not of fact. In point of fact, I think you have made a most interesting and important assemblage of the essential points to be considered in connection with the Battle of New Orleans, and have shown conclusively that the opinion so frequently expressed by historians, that the battle was unnecessary, is a sentimental inaccuracy which ought to be corrected. You have done a useful and important piece of work, and I congratulate you upon its completion.

May I beg you to be good enough to favor me with a copy when the work is printed? I should like to prepare a review of it for one of our local newspapers.

Yours very truly,
JOHN S. KENDALL.

DETAILS OF RESEARCH

CRUSADE SWORD.

VOLTAIRE, FRENCH CYNIC, IS QUOTED AS SAYING THAT HISTORY IS MADE UP OF LIES AGREED UPON. HERE IS ONE ALMOST AGREED UPON, NOW OVERHAULED AND EXPOSED.

LOUISIANA DOMAIN.

The Louisiana spoken of in this volume refers to the great Louisiana Domain purchased by President Jefferson from France in 1803. That original Domain now comprehends all or most of sixteen states, as follows: Arkansas, Colorado, Idaho, Iowa, Kansas, Louisiana, Minnesota, Missouri, Montana, Nebraska, North Dakota, Oklahoma, Oregon, South Dakota, Washington and Wyoming.

CHAPTER I.

AN INTERVIEW CONTAINING AN OUTLINE.

It was the 8th of January. I sat down for lunch at a small table in a Nashville hotel. Presently the head waiter conducted to a seat opposite me a young man, seemingly about 22 years of age. He was a handsome, wholesome looking young man, and had an air of self-reliance. He impressed me at first sight as being a typical young American; at any rate he was decidedly attractive to the narrator, whose grey head could but reveal his advanced years.

While awaiting the lunches, a casual remark about the weather opened conversation. A waiter brought an afternoon paper. On the front page was a picture of Andrew Jackson, and big headlines over accounts of celebrations in memory of the victory at New Orleans in 1815.

The young man, with the superiority of youthful knowledge, exclaimed:

"Why all this to-do about a battle which was a needless one? It was a brilliant victory, and salved American pride at the time; but that is now four generations in the past. We should not go on salving our pride over a useless victory, and especially when it was over a country now our strong and perpetual friend. We don't need anything to boost our pride any more. We are now the greatest nation on earth."

While responding to the fervor in the young man's last sentence, I felt a kind of joy in his prelude, which I knew was based on history that I knew to be false.

In brief explanation, let me say that for some years, I have been engaged in research work as to the true value of the battle of New Orleans, resulting in the conviction that the current appraisal in school histories is entirely erroneous. I therefore welcomed the opportunity to develop the truth to this typical young American. I decided upon the gradual approach rather than a frontal attack, which might result in amour propre resentment.

I said in a casual tone:

"Permit me to take issue with you. Suppose I should tell you that the Battle of New Orleans was not a needless battle; that it was, in fact, the second most important military event in the life of our republic? Suppose I should say to you that it was not fought after peace, but during war?"

The young man looked at me, first with a show of impatience, and then with a tolerant air.

"My only answer," he returned, "is that you haven't read our modern histories. I have. The Peace Treaty of Ghent was signed Christmas Eve, 1814. Sailing vessels were the quickest means of communication at that time, and so it was more than six weeks before the news reached our people. During that interim the Battle of New Orleans was fought. So you see it was quite useless except as a contribution to American pride."

"Have you read that treaty?" I asked.

"Sure," he responded, "that is, I have read several reliable digests. They all say the treaty was silent as to Impressment and Orders in Council, which caused our declaration of war, and that it amounted to a simple agreement to stop fighting and go back to the status before the war."

As I was calculating on my next move the young man resumed:

"We had a debate at school last year on the question, 'Resolved, that the United States won the War of 1812.' I took the ground that it was a draw, and my side won. So you can see that I am well posted on that war."

He had a polite, patronizing air, and this decided me upon a direct blow.

"I thank you," said I; "I have also closely studied the events of this War of 1812. I have read some more or less superficial comments on the Peace Treaty of Ghent. I have also read the Treaty itself, word by word. In precise specific terms, that document stipulated that it was not to be effective until ratified by both sides."

The young man gave an inquiring look, and commented:

"That of course is important, if true."

"It is true," I replied. "You can verify the fact in fifteen minutes. A few blocks from where we sit is a Carnegie Library in which you can find a volume containing various treaties of the United States. The Treaty of Ghent is among them. It is called the Treaty of Amity."

"May I ask who you are?" questioned the young man, with a changed and puzzled mien.

"I am a member of the Committee appointed by the State to make research into the real value of the Battle of New Orleans."

"I am delighted to know you," said the young man. "I love to discuss history, which reveals the foundation of our existing social structure. There are some questions I would like to ask of you. First, since the Treaty was eventually ratified, aren't our historians while technically wrong, in saying the Battle of New Orleans occurred after Peace, and was a useless battle, really in the right, for the reason that the battle really had no effect upon the Peace Treaty?"

"It is true," I replied, "the Treaty adopted at Ghent, Dec. 24, 1814, was ratified soon after its reception in Washington, and promulgated the next day, Feb. 18, 1815. That was after the news of the victory at New Orleans had reached Washington.

"But suppose the result at New Orleans had been different, would President

Madison have signed the Treaty?

"That is a real question for college debate. It is a question calculated to bring sharply to the student the picture of the distracted condition of our country at the time. By signing the treaty Madison would have appeased the New England section, then in hostile and threatening attitude, but at the same time would have faced the surrender of the territory west of the Mississippi for all time, or faced future negotiation or war. By refusing to sign, the President would have prolonged the war with its uncertainties. At the same time he would have confronted possible disunion through the open disaffection of the northeastern states. The English government construed the disaffection as a threat of secession.

"It was planned by that calculating government, as evidence shows, to inveigle New England into a separate treaty in case after British capture and occupation of New Orleans, Madison should refuse to ratify the Ghent treaty. Thus, if the issue in that New Orleans affair had been different, President Madison would have faced danger of disunion, on one side or the other.

"It would be hard to conceive of a graver situation. All this was averted, and gloriously averted, by the victory at New Orleans, the news of which caused the treaty to be joyfully ratified."

"Haven't you overdrawn the picture?" asked the young man. "Isn't it a fact that the treaty provided for the return of all territory taken during the war, so that, if the English had captured New Orleans they would have given it up?"

"My dear young friend," I replied, "I have not overdrawn the picture. The mutual restoration clause provided that all territory, places and possessions, taken by either, were to be returned at effective peace. Bear in mind that England had never conceded the validity of our title to the Louisiana Domain, and so if the carefully planned design to capture it had been successful, England was in position to hold that she did not regard it as a legal possession of the United States, and as not subject to return under the Peace Treaty. It is a violence to credibility to suppose that England, after finally dispatching the big expedition against Louisiana, would within a few weeks thereafter, agree to a peace treaty, recalling her troops from an anticipated successful conquest. In the light of present knowledge, the peace proceedings show a studied purpose to protect the expedition sent out to capture New Orleans. The supposition, advanced by many historians, that if England had captured New Orleans, she would have given it up, is a reflection upon the intelligence of the English government of that period, and really, ascribes to that government egregious asininity. Now, with all of her blunders, England has never been asinine."

The young man listened intently, gave an inhaled "Oh," and then added:

"I begin to see; but there are some questions I want to ask. First, when and why and how did this error get in history?"

"A natural inquiry," I responded. "I cannot definitely answer, nor is a definite answer vital. However, I will give one conjecture; Jackson became a national figure as a result of the Battle of New Orleans. While acclaimed by the masses, Jackson had many bitter enemies, some of them in the history writing class. Prejudice may have caused disparagement of the importance of the event upon which his national fame is founded. But all that is of small importance beside the establishment of the actual truth, that the battle was not fought after peace, but that it was necessary to prevent England's conquest of Louisiana. Thus, as I have said before, the Battle was the second most important military event in the life of the Republic."

"Now my other questions," said the young man; "why has such an error been allowed to go unchallenged all these generations?"

"Another natural question," I answered. "It is a question that must come to every mind in approaching this matter of clarification. I am not able to answer this question definitely, just as I was not able to answer your other question with any degree of certainty. The answer is not vital, except from the standpoint of the problem involved, of overcoming the inertia of a long-enthroned lie. My conjecture is that the false appraisal began when civil upheaval was imminent, and when most people were thinking only of the present—a state of mind which was continued for a long time. So the viewpoint of prejudice, unopposed, gradually crept into accepted history. There have been, and are, students of history adhering to the great fact that the Battle of New Orleans saved the Louisiana purchase, or another war with England. But school histories continue to purvey the false viewpoint to the youth of the land. But 'truth is mighty and will prevail,' and the time has now come."

At this point a bell boy brought me a card, and I arose to bid goodbye to my young friend, saying;

"They have come for me, to go to the Hermitage for the exercises being held there today."

The young man said:

"I wish it were so you could take me."

I arranged to do so, very much pleased at this change in his attitude.

CHAPTER II.

CONTAINING A HIGH COMMISSION AND AN IN-DICTMENT.

There is no nobler calling than that of the school teachers of America, who are ministering to the instruction and development of the future citizens and leaders of the Republic. These teachers are bound to be deeply concerned when they find that through school histories furnished them, they have been imparting a falsehood about an important event in United States history—the Battle of New Orleans, fought January 8, 1815. These school histories minimize the value of the battle, describing it as needless, because fought after peace, when as a fact, the battle was not fought after peace, and the victory, in fact, prevented a carefully planned conquest of the then lately acquired Louisiana Domain, with all the attendant, untoward complications, another war being one of them.

It is the purpose of this volume to show by reliable authorities, the truth as to the value of this battle.

History, as is well known, is honey-combed with lies, originally projected either in ignorance, prejudice or adulation. We are always fortunate if able to arrest and correct one before too late.

The Legislature of Tennessee, at its session of 1927, adopted the following resolution:

"WHEREAS, the Battle of New Orleans, fought on January 8, 1815, is one of the outstanding military events of American History; and,

"WHEREAS, the memory of the great American victory achieved there, is especially cherished by Tennesseans because of Andrew Jackson, and the other Tennesseans who therein immortalized themselves; and,

"WHEREAS, school histories, adopted for and taught in our schools, convey the impression that the battle was a needless one in that it occurred fifteen days after the treaty of Peace had been signed at Ghent, Belgium, by the Commissioners representing the United States and England; and,

"WHEREAS, serious criticism is made that such textbooks present an erroneous appraisement of the value of the battle, by omitting the reference to an essential fact, to-wit: that England did not construe the Peace Treaty of Ghent as applicable to Louisiana, for the reason that she held as invalid the title of the United States to that Domain, conveyed by Napoleon Bonaparte in 1803; and,

"WHEREAS, it is of prime importance that our school children should receive every essential truth from historical textbooks, and especially those textbooks placed in the hands of Tennessee students should portray in its true significance the battle of New Orleans in which the ancestors of so many were engaged; Now,

"THEREFORE, be it resolved by the Senate, the House of Representatives concurring, that the Governor be, and is hereby empowered and authorized, to appoint five, or in his discretion seven, persons of known historical knowledge and research, who shall constitute a Commission, charged with the duty of carefully examining the authorities, touching the true value of the Battle of New Orleans, fought January 8, 1815; and,

"Said Commission shall incorporate its conclusions and recommendations in a report to the Governor who shall transmit the same to the Legislature."

The present writer, who was appointed a member of the authorized Committee, has been engaged in making research into the matter involved, and has found facts, not hard of access, which should, and will, when understood, force a radical revision of school histories in the version they present as to the value of the New Orleans victory.

Other members of the Commission appointed by the Governor were: John H. DeWitt, of Nashville, Judge of the Tennessee Court of Appeals and president of the Tennessee Historical Society; John Trotwood Moore, of Nashville, State Librarian and historian; Claude G. Bowers, New York, author, historian, and editor—now ambassador to Spain; John S. Kendall, of New Orleans, historian and professor in Tulane University.

It is the purpose of the writer, after submission for comment to his distinguished fellow Committeemen, to make this volume the basis of report to the Governor of Tennessee for transmission to the Legislature.

In order to present, in as simple a way as possible, the case, or the indictment, for such it is, actual and authenticated excerpts are given herewith from all the American histories prescribed for Tennessee Public Schools by the State Text Book Commission.

These extracts were obtained from the office of the Secretary of State, where under statute, copies of all adopted text books are kept.

CHAPTER III.

WHAT SCHOOL HISTORIES TEACH.

Here are the extracts from the Tennessee authorized school Histories:

School History of Tennessee: S. E. Scates, page 225:

"Though the battle resulted in great victory for the Americans, it was sad indeed that so many brave men lost their lives at New Orleans quite uselessly. At Ghent, Belgium, a treaty of peace for the war of 1812 had been signed Christmas Eve, 1814. Because messages travelled so slowly, by sailing vessels, news of peace did not reach New Orleans until after the fighting had taken place."

A History of American Government and Culture: Harold Rugg, page 192:

"Two weeks after the Treaty of Peace had been signed, another battle was fought. This may seem strange to you, but in those days transportation and communication was so slow that news of the making of peace reached the country long after it had happened."

History of the United States: Beard & Beard, page 238:

"The Treaty of Peace. Both countries were in truth sick of a war that offered neither glory nor profit. So after an exchange of notes they sent representatives to Ghent to discuss a settlement. Long negotiations were finally ended by an agreement on Christmas Eve, 1814, a few days before Jackson's victory at New Orleans. When the treaty reached America the people were surprised to find it said nothing about the seizure of American sailors, the destruction of American trade, the searching for American ships, or the support of Indians on the frontier. Nevertheless, we are told, the public 'passed from gloom to glory' on the arrival of the news of peace. Bells were rung; schools were closed; flags were displayed; and many a rousing toast was drunk in taverns and private homes. The rejoicing could continue. With Napoleon definitely beaten at Waterloo in June, 1815, Great Britain had no more need to impress sailors, search ships, and seize American goods bound to the Continent. Once more the terrible sea power sank into the background and the ocean was again white with the sails of merchantmen."

History of the American People: Latane, page 284:

"Jackson's brilliant victory at the Battle of New Orleans caused great rejoicing throughout the country, but it did not affect the outcome of the war, for the treaty of peace had been signed at Ghent two weeks before it was fought. Its effect on the course of American history, however, was far-reaching, for it brought the West into greater prominence and made Andrew Jackson the military hero and political leader of that section."

A History of the People of the United States: Waddy Thompson, page 220:

"Treaty of Peace; Results of the War: The great victory of New Orleans was won after peace had been made. A treaty had been signed at Ghent, Belgium, on December 24, 1814. But as only sailing vessels then crossed the ocean, and as about six weeks were required for the voyage, news of peace did not reach America until February, 1815."

First Book in United States History: Waddy Thompson, page 253:

"A Victory after Peace: Brilliant as was the victory at New Orleans, it was won after peace had been made between the United States and Great Britain. Both sides having become tired of the War, a treaty of peace was signed in Belgium in December, 1814; while the Battle of New Orleans was fought on January 8, 1815. Steamboats did not then cross the Ocean, and no electric cable connected America with Europe, so news of the treaty did not reach America until a month after the Battle of New Orleans."

The American People: Muzzey, page 218:

"Jackson, henceforth, the 'Hero of New Orleans' was rewarded in the following years by the command against the Indians of Florida (1817), the governorship of Florida territory (1821); a seat in the United States Senate (1823), and the Presidency of the United States (1829). If the Atlantic cable had existed in 1814, it would have brought the news of the treaty of peace in time to turn Pakenham's expedition back from the Mississippi, to prevent the bloodiest battle that had ever been fought on American soil, and perhaps to keep from the pages of American history the administration of the most masterful of our Presidents between Washington and Lincoln."

CHAPTER IV.

FALSEHOOD SHOWN BY THE RECORDS.

The unanimity of view presented by these extracts from Tennessee adopted histories, gives justification for the assumption that the same view obtains throughout the United States. In partial extenuation of school historians and of Textbook Commissions, it may be said that they have followed the lead of most generally recognized historians. But any trusting follower of the pack leaders could have ascertained, without much trouble, that the battle of New Orleans was NOT fought after peace. It occurred fifteen days after the Treaty of Ghent had been signed by the Commissioners of the two interested nations, but expressly, by the terms of that treaty, it was not to be effective until ratified by both sides and ratification exchanged in Washington.

Let us go to specific quotations. The Peace Treaty of Ghent, dated December 24, 1814, contained, as its first sentence, the following words: "All hostilities, both by sea and by land shall cease as soon as this treaty shall be ratified by both parties as hereinafter mentioned."

Article XI of the Treaty reads: "This Treaty, when the same shall be ratified on both sides, without alteration by either of the contracting parties, and the ratification mutually exchanged, shall be binding on both parties; and the ratification shall be exchanged at Washington, in the space of four months from this date, or sooner if practicable."

Further, the record shows that ratification of the Treaty was advised by the United States Senate, February 16, 1815; that it was ratified February 17; and ratification exchanged the same day, and that it was promulgated February 18th.

The Treaty of Ghent, called the Treaty of Amity, is preserved, of course, among American State papers. A copy may be found in a public library in a volume devoted to Treaties, Agreements, Etc. between the U. S. A. and other Powers, Compiled by W. M. Maloy, Under Resolution of U. S. Senate of Jan. 18, 1909.

A lawyer friend of the writer, with whom he discussed the situation, suggested that while manifestly in error in representing the Battle as having been fought after peace, that a plea in abatement might be offered for the historians to the effect that the treaty was subsequently ratified as written; that the Battle of New Orleans had no effect upon the Treaty; that it further was needless because if its issue had been different the British under the mutual restoration clause of the Ghent Treaty would, upon promulgation of the Treaty, have evacuated New Orleans and Louisiana.

That viewpoint is entitled to such consideration as should be given any viewpoint based solely on assumption, but it and all such viewpoints must be subjected to acid judgment based on co-related facts.

As to the first point above made, it is a matter of record that the treaty was ratified quickly after reaching Washington; it is also a matter of record that the news of the great American victory at New Orleans reached the Capitol ten days before. As to the second point, that the battle had no effect upon the treaty, a wide range of discussion, based on records, is opened, which will be presented later.

As to the third point, that the battle was needless because, if successful, the British would have evacuated New Orleans and Louisiana upon promulgation of the Peace Treaty, it may be stated here that the records which will be presently laid before the reader give decided negation to that assumption.

The writer boldly avers, as supported truth, that the British Government, never having acknowledged the validity of the title of the United States to Louisiana, secretly dispatched the big expedition against New Orleans with one hand, while directing peace negotiations with the other; that it was the British purpose to seize and hold Louisiana, nominally in the name of Spain; and that the British Government would never have agreed to a peace treaty, which did not contain a clause, no matter how subtly garbed, that would not give justification to the British retention of Louisiana.

However, before going into the matter of citations of authorities and records, it is due to the reader to present something of the English attitude at the time, so that he may see more clearly and with more understanding its actions. That can best be done by brief picture of the background of that period.

CHAPTER V.

BACKGROUND—LOUISIANA.

The great domain, christened Louisiana, was taken over by La Salle in 1682, in the name of France. It remained under French dominion until 1763, when, as a result of French-English wars, France retired from the New World. It seemed inevitable that Louisiana, great unexplored trans-river territory, would fall into English hands. But France ceded Louisiana to Spain, then still a world power. In 1800 Napoleon Bonaparte caused Spain to re-cede Louisiana to France. In 1803 Bonaparte sold Louisiana to the United States. He was about to engage in war with England, and historians generally agree that the sale to United States was made because he recognized the difficulty of defending the remote territory against the English Navy. The British Encyclopedia says the sale was made to keep Louisiana from falling into English hands. Thus it appears, that England was justified in feeling that Louisiana for the second time had been maneuvered from her ownership.

References without number may be given from histories covering that period. The writer has before him James G. Blaine's "Twenty Years in Congress," which in Chapter 1 of the first volume (pages 3 to 13) deals comprehensively with the relation of the Louisiana purchase to the early days of the Republic. Some key quotations are here presented: "She (France) in 1763, now gave up Canada and Cape Breton, acknowledged the sovereignty of Great Britain in the original thirteen colonies as extending to the Mississippi, and, by a separate treaty, surrendered Louisiana on the west side of the Mississippi, with New Orleans on the east side, to Spain. She (Spain) continued in possession of Louisiana until the year 1800, when Bonaparte concluded a Treaty ..., by which the entire territory was retroceded to France."

Again, Mr. Blaine says: "Fearing that in the threatening conflict (1803) England, by her superior Naval force, would deprive him of his newly acquired colonial empire, and greatly enhance her own prestige by securing all the American possessions, which France had owned prior to 1763, Bonaparte, by a dash in diplomacy, as quick and as brilliant as his tactics on the field of battle, placed Louisiana beyond the reach of the British power. In a tone of vehemence and passion he said: 'I know the full value of Louisiana. A few lines of a treaty have restored it to me, and now I must expect to lose it. The English expect to take possession of it, and it is thus they will begin the war. They have already twenty ships of the line in the Gulf of Mexico. The conquest of Louisiana will be easy. I have not a moment to lose in putting it out of their reach. The English have successively taken from France the Canadas, Cape Breton, Newfoundland, Nova Scotia, and the richest portion of Asia. But they shall not have the Mississippi, which they covet.'"

Again quoting from Blaine: "England's acquisition of Louisiana would have proved in the highest degree embarrassing, if not disastrous to the Union. No colonial acquisition ever made by her on any continent has been so profitable to her commerce, and so strengthening to her military position, as that of Louisiana would have proved. The fact was clearly seen by Bonaparte when he hastily made the treaty ceding it to the United States."

Again Blaine: "The conflict of arms (War of 1812) did not occur until nine years after; and it is a curious and not unimportant fact, that the most notable defeat of the British troops in the second war of independence, as the struggle of 1812 has been well named, occurred on the soil of the territory for whose protection the original precaution had been taken by Jefferson."

The reader will find all of the chapter referred to very interesting as indeed will be any chapter devoted to our sudden acquisition of the immense domain called Louisiana.

The striking sentences quoted above serve to emphasize the fact that it would not have been unnatural for England to have felt resentment at this second maneuvering of a vast territory from her grasp. Some historians have expressed surprise that England did not at once undertake to take Louisiana, the United States notwithstanding. That would have meant armed conflict with America at a time of the war in Europe. Besides, and this is a deduction of the present writer, such a course would have placed upon England the onus before the world of a war of conquest in the western continent. So England waited.

An additional viewpoint is here presented: In the history of the United States of America, by Henry W. Elson, under the caption "Louisiana" (Vol. 2, page 230) appears the following paragraph (page 233): "Actual possession soon placed our title to Louisiana beyond dispute; but strictly speaking, the sale was not legal. Napoleon had agreed to convey to Spain a dukedom on the Arno River, for the son-in-law of the Spanish King, in payment for Louisiana; but the price was never paid. The treaty of Ildefonso also stipulated that France should never cede the territory to any foreign power; but Napoleon disregarded this. In point of fact, France, therefore, did not own Louisiana; and even if she had owned it, the cession, according to the French Constitution, could not be made without the consent of the Chamber of Deputies, and this the First Consul never obtained and never sought. The French people were astonished at this action of their ruler; but he was a master, and they were powerless. Far sadder was the wail from Spain. The Spanish Government protested briefly, pathetically; but its voice was not heard."

From the above quotation the reader can appreciate England's attitude, as to the legality of the United States' title to Louisiana, maintained until January 8, 1815, when the highest law known to nations dissipated that attitude forever.

There are doubtless many today, as we bask in the enjoyment of National security and other national blessings, who do not appreciate the vastness, the importance, of the Louisiana domain, the acquisition of which Dr. Sloane of Princeton says translated our young republic into a world power. According to an early authority the domain comprised 829,987 square miles, and by later authority over a million square miles. In the Louisiana Purchase territory are today comprehended the following states: Arkansas, Colorado, Idaho, Iowa, Kansas, Louisiana, Minnesota, Missouri, Montana, Nebraska, North Dakota, Oklahoma, Oregon, South Dakota, Washington and Wyoming.

CHAPTER VI.

BACKGROUND—IMPRESSMENT.

The impressment policy of the English Government applied to the new American country, was very galling. Under that policy American ships were stopped on the high seas, and seamen taken from them under guise of being British deserters. Many good Americans were forced into British service. The young victim country protested. In 1801 the impressment practice fell off and seemingly was abandoned. (See Elson's History of the U. S., pages 246 to 252, Vol. 2.) A quotation is given from Elson, page 247, Vol. 2: "This (impressment) practice had fallen into the background during the short season of peace between France and England, that ended in 1803, but with the renewal of the war it had been revived with alarming vigor."

Whether that "alarming vigor" was due entirely to war exigencies of recruiting its Navy, or whether the British Government designed it as a provocation to the young western Republic, to take the onus of declaring war, under guise of which the coveted floating title to Louisiana could be appropriated, is a matter for deduction, not appearing of record.

At any rate, the impressment practice re-aroused resentment in the young republic, and that resentment found chief expression in the then Southwest, resulting under the leadership of that section and over the opposition of the New England States, or rather of that of the assertive Federalists therein, in a declaration of war against England, on the ground of the degradation of our sovereignty.

It is not the purpose of the writer to discuss the War of 1812, except as its events may relate to his mission, that of correcting falsehood and error in the historical books adopted as textbooks for the school children of America.

The War of 1812 was heralded as a mistake by the Federalists, opponents of the then administration. While the incipient Navy gave a brilliant account of itself, justifying the proud boast that man for man and gun for gun, the U. S. Navy was the equal of anything afloat, for two and a half years the record shows that land events in the main were untoward, climaxed by the capture, and sacking and burning of the public buildings, of the National Capital in August, 1814, and thus the Federal Press offensively took the "I-told-you-so" attitude.

Early in the war the Emperor of Russia extended his good offices as mediator. The United States Government accepted the offer, being earnestly desirous of honorable peace, and having nothing to conceal from neutral investigation. But the English government declined the Russian offer, indicating that it preferred to treat direct. Later as a result of British invitation, a Peace Commission met at

Ghent, Belgium.

CHAPTER VII.

NEGOTIATIONS AT GHENT.

A separate chapter is devoted to the joint conference at Ghent because therein is shown the subtle, diplomatically concealed, purpose of the then English Government. The record of the proceedings of the conference, in order to be fully understood, should be read in the light of the afterwards revealed fact that, at the same time these negotiations were being conducted, the expedition against Louisiana was secretly planned and dispatched. Things that are puzzling in the making often become clear in the aftermath. And so it is in this case.

The defeat and resultant abdication of Napoleon (April 4, 1814) released England's European troops for pursuing the American war with greater vigor, and to punish the United States for having declared war at England's most embarrassing moment. It would not be a violent assumption to say that at least some members of the British Government felt that the time was opportune at last to take Louisiana and thus redress a grievance nurtured since 1803, when Bonaparte snatched that great domain from England's outstretched hands.

The exact date on which the Louisiana expedition was determined upon is not material. Plain evidence discloses that during the joint peace negotiation its details were arranged and the army sent forward to take New Orleans. We now know that after the capture of Washington by the British and the burning and sacking of the public buildings there (August 24, 1814), the British invading forces, after being later repulsed in an attack upon Baltimore, repaired under orders to Nigril Bay, Jamaica, to await recruits for the expedition against New Orleans. With the time then required for ocean travel, these orders must have been given prior to, or about the time of the meeting of the Peace Commissioners at Ghent, August 4, 1814.

Let us visualize the two groups assembled at Ghent. First, consider the five Americans. They were earnestly desirous of a quick and honorable peace. Their country was riven with dissatisfaction produced by a powerful anti-administration and anti-war party, seemingly in control of the northeastern states, making dire threats, unless hostilities were soon ended.

The American Commissioners were prepared and authorized to forego the questions of impressment and orders in council, which caused the war, and conclude a peace pact on the basis of the status before the war. For a month they had been waiting the coming of the British Commissioners. It is evident there was a purpose on the part of the British Government to delay.

The second group consisted of three suave English Commissioners, who appeared at Ghent, as before stated, August 4th.

These English Commissioners began by making, on behalf of their Government, demands objectionable and humiliating, the discussion of which, often at long distance with the London Government officials, consumed time. Finally the American Commissioners were forced to write to Washington for further instructions.

From "The Diplomacy of the War of 1812," by Frank A. Updyke, which is a most valuable account of the Peace conference, quotation is given from pages 220 and 221. "It was the unanimous opinion of the American ministers that Great Britain's policy was to consume as much time as possible before the termination of negotiations, in order that some decided victory might be gained in the war which would make it easier for her to insist upon her demands."

This quotation is given to show that our ministers recognized the British tactics as sparring for time; but the record does not show that any one of them thought of New Orleans as the objective point of British design.

The records in connection with the negotiations are voluminous, and make very interesting reading. But viewed in the after revealed facts, the truth stands out so clearly that the proceedings of the Peace Conference in English consideration and the secret expedition to capture New Orleans were so closely inter-related that in arriving at the material verity, much material in that conference should be disregarded as intended by the English to delay and becloud, and so matters coming before the Conference referring to Louisiana should only be considered in connection with our mission.

Frank A. Updyke, Ph.D. of Dartmouth College, in his "The Diplomacy of the War of 1812," quoted from above, has given a condensed, fully annotated, account of the proceedings of the Peace Conference. It is a work, published in 1915, which deserves place as a supplementary textbook in every college and high school. I have made liberal use of Dr. Updyke's volume, which merits high place for research effort and reference.

The Joint Commission had been in session a little over two months when the first note was struck significant of the British underlying purpose. It was in the communication of the English Government through their ministers to the American Commissioners. The document was dated October 8, 1814. (See American State papers.)

"The first paragraph," says Updyke (page 269), "attempted to show the illegality of the purchase of Louisiana and the spirit of territorial aggrandisement on the part of the United States which this act manifested."

It might have been inferred that this attack upon the legality of the title to Louisiana would be followed by a demand of some sort; but no such demand was made. In fact, the treaty as finally adopted, contained no mention of Louisiana.

It is highly pertinent to ask a question as to what was the purpose of this attack upon the title of Louisiana. All such things have a purpose.

In the light of present knowledge that purpose is clear. The great expedition against New Orleans being near completion, it is obvious that the British Government recognized the good diplomatic position before the world, after the capture of Louisiana, of showing a record of fair warning as justification for retention.

The reply of the Americans to the note of October 8th was dated October 13th. (See American State papers.)

Quotation is given from Updyke, page 284:

"While endeavoring to make the reply brief, the American ministers could not refrain from discussing some other topics adverted to by the British in their note. The British ministers had made the charge that the acquisition of Louisiana by the United States was illegal, Spain having offered a remonstrance against its cession and the right of France to make it. To this the American note responded that, although the Spanish minister at Washington had made such remonstrance, at that very time orders were given by Spain for the delivery of Louisiana to France. So France was in actual possession of the territory when she disposed of it to the United States."

Another matter, although not in chronological turn, may be here presented, as showing further the English attitude towards Louisiana. In the course of the note of the Americans to the British, dated November 10, 1814 (see American State papers), Updyke says, page 307: "The American note refused to consent to the British proposal to fix the northwest boundary by the line from the lake of the Woods to the Mississippi unless the boundaries of Louisiana should also be provided for in the settlement."

The British ministers in referring the note to their Government, said they were unwilling to consent to a discussion of the Louisiana boundary, for their doing so might be taken as a recognition of the right of the United States to the occupation of the territory. (See Updyke, page 310.)

What might be called the Uti Possidetis scheme was embraced in a British note of October 21st (see American State papers). The British proposed the Uti Possidetis principle, as a basis of settlement, under which each side would keep what territory it should be possessed of at the promulgation of peace.

The reason behind this proposal seems now very patent. The adoption of this principle would have enabled England, by indisputable treaty right, to retain Louisiana, which she confidently expected to take.

But the Americans opposed this principle and firmly insisted on a treaty based upon conditions at the beginning of the war.

The English were very insistent and for a time there appeared a new danger that the conference would break up. But, as will appear later, British diplomacy, the most skilful in the world, found a way to accomplish the main objective of the Uti Possidetis; that is to say, the retention of Louisiana after the expected reduction of New Orleans.

While these peace negotiations were simmering at Ghent, the well-planned, secret expedition against New Orleans was completed in detail, and with confident feeling of assurance that, because of its size and veteran fibre, it would be invincible, it was finally put on its way to join the waiting troops at Nigril Bay, Jamaica. Sir Edward Pakenham was appointed Commander of the Expeditionary forces. A. C. Buell, in his "History of Andrew Jackson," published in 1904, states that Pakenham's order was dated November 4, 1814, and read according to English war office minute; that General Pakenham "shall proceed to Plymouth and embark there for Louisiana to assume command of the forces operating for the reduction of that province." Buell cites as authority Bathurst papers; State Paper Office, London.

On the assumption of the correctness of Buell's citation, the term "Province" as applied to Louisiana, in English official orders, represents the radical difference of viewpoint as to Louisiana at the time between the British Government and the American Union, of which the English termed province was a fair possession from which already one state had been carved. (Louisiana in 1812.)

While the British Expedition was ploughing the seas, unexpected resistance was forming under an American general, who didn't know what defeat was.

CHAPTER VIII.

NEGOTIATIONS AT GHENT—CONTINUED.

We will now return to the parleys at Ghent. The British continued to insist on the Uti Possidetis as a basis of a Peace Treaty, but proposed that it be "subject to such modifications as mutual convenience may be found to require." In a letter to the British Commissioners, dated October 18th, Lord Bathurst, quoted by Updyke (page 288), cited several points on which mutual accommodations might be had; but Louisiana was not one of the points. For if it had been there would have seemingly been no use planning and sending out the great expedition for the "reduction of that province."

From many interesting details touching the Uti Possidetis proposals, the reader is referred to Updyke ("The Diplomacy of the War of 1812"), pages 288 to 319.

Finally, realizing the unshaken adherence of the Americans to the antebellum status, the British gave up the Uti Possidetis demand, and by specific wording obviously sought to protect the Louisiana design.

In the amended proposal of the British (see British to American ministers Nov. 26, 1814), there are two things highly pertinent to the inquiry we are conducting, to establish the real value of the Battle of New Orleans. The first was the provision that peace would not be effective until after ratification by both countries. The second consisted in the proposed wording for the mutual restoration clause as follows: "Belonging to either party, taken by the other." The effect of this wording in the mutual restoration clause, would have been that all territory belonging to either party, taken by the other, should be returned. But this would not embrace Louisiana, for from the English standpoint, it did not legally belong to the United States.

As to the first point, a quotation is here given from Updyke (page 317): "The amended project returned by the British commissioners provided that the notification for the cessation of the war be issued after ratifications of the treaty should have been exchanged rather than at the time of the signature. This was designed, it was supposed, to give time for the completion of the British plans against New Orleans, the successful outcome of which was never doubted."

The American ministers, on November 30th, consented to the substitution of the day of exchange of ratifications for that of the signature of the treaty, as the time for cessation of hostilities, and for regulating the period when prizes at sea shall be restored. (See American to British ministers, Nov. 30, 1814.)

This agreement was duly carried into the treaty, as we have heretofore set forth, Article XI, prescribing all details.

The American ministers opposed the proposed words in the mutual restoration clause, "belonging to either party, taken by the other." They insisted on the words, "taken by either party from the other." Strong reasons were given by the Americans for their attitude, but the British ministers refused to yield, saying the matter would be referred to their Government (Updyke, pp. 324-325).

The British Government, on December 6th, instructed their Commissioners to insist upon the retention of the words in dispute, and advanced skilful arguments, in which the real purpose was not revealed. For a digest of these arguments, see Updyke, pages 335-336.

To the present day reader, having knowledge of the expedition, which was then on its way to capture New Orleans, the English purpose seems very manifest.

With diplomatic art the British Government sought to make it appear that the disputed words, "belonging to either party and taken by the other," were founded in the objective relating to the islands in Passamaquoddy Bay during the time of the agreed upon reference to a commission to determine the ownership of these Islands.

The Americans, not aware, of course, of the expedition against New Orleans, accepted the viewpoint advanced as to the disputed words, but while rejecting the words, indicated that they would be "willing to admit such a modification as should secure the right of Great Britain from being affected or impaired by yielding possession of the Islands to the United States." (Updyke, p. 343.)

The British ministers replied, arguing England's position. That position in effect was, that during the war she had taken these islands, the title to which was in dispute, and that to call upon her to restore them, because they were occupied by the United States at the beginning of the war, would be unjust; that having agreed to a commission to settle the ownership of the islands, she was willing, if need be, to accede to a clause which would especially guard the ultimate right against the prejudice which the American ministers feared might arise from the continued possession by Great Britain. The British ministers admitted the comparatively small value of the territory in question, but claimed that yielding possession of the Islands involved a point of honor on the part of Great Britain, and, if insisted upon, might make the conclusion of peace impossible. (See Updyke, pp. 343-344; report of conference of Dec. 12, 1814, given by British Commissioners to Lord Castlereagh.)

The Americans yielded the point, and thus it appears that the British Government secured the accession of the principle of the great concealed objective on a matter of minor importance. Thus the word "possessions" was admitted into the mutual restoration clause of the peace treaty.

That mutual restoration clause, as adopted, and incorporated in Article 1, of the Treaty of Ghent, reads as follows:

"All territory, places and possessions whatsoever, taken by either party from the other during the War, or which may be taken after the signing of this Treaty, excepting only the Islands hereinafter mentioned, shall be restored without delay and without causing any destruction or carrying away of any of the artillery or other public property originally captured in the said forts or places, and which shall remain therein upon the exchange of the ratification of this Treaty, or any slaves or other private property; and all archives, records, deeds, and papers, either of a public nature or belonging to private persons, which, in the course of the War, may have fallen into the hands of the officers, of either party shall be, as far as may be practicable, forthwith restored and delivered to the proper authorities and persons to whom they respectively belong. Such of the Islands in the Bay of Passamaquoddy as are claimed by both parties, shall remain in the possession of the party in whose occupation they may be at the time of the exchange of the ratification of this Treaty until the decision respecting the title to said islands shall have been made in conformity with the fourth article of this Treaty. No disposition made by this Treaty as to such possession of such islands and territories claimed by both parties shall, in any manner whatever, be construed to affect the right of either."

The Treaty, from which the clause above is quoted, can of course be found in Washington, but copy may be seen at almost any general public library, in the volume herebefore referred to containing various Treaties of the United States.

The reader, who has been following us in our showing of the various stages of the development of the British design to protect, by diplomacy, the Louisiana expedition, will recognize the significance of the word "possessions." By reason of that word, the British were in position to maintain, after capturing Louisiana, that it was not subject to return under the mutual restoration clause adopted, not being, under English construction, a legal "possession" of the United States, formal notice of that construction having been given in the treaty negotiations. The subtly accomplished insertion of the word in the treaty represented a triumph of ulterior British diplomatic design over the very able, hard-headed, but open and candid American commissioners, who were entirely in the dark as to the Expedition dispatched to seize Louisiana.

That word was of course not as exclusive of argument as the Uti Possidetis principle first proposed, and insisted upon almost as a sine qua non; nor was it as clear as the wording subsequently urged, "belonging to either party and taken by the other"; but it was all sufficient, backed by the British conviction that Louisiana was not a legal possession of the United States, and supported by the mighty British martial power, then unleashed from European war.

It is obvious to the writer that but for the word "possessions," or wording of similar import, the treaty would not have been agreed to by the British; in fact, such indication was given by the British ministers at the joint conference December 12th, under the guise of the principle pertaining to the Passamaquoddy Islands.

Any presumption that Great Britain, after planning the great expedition against Louisiana, would have, within a few weeks following the final dispatch of the military forces, signed a peace treaty, recalling those forces from an attained, long-dreamed-of conquest, is a reflection upon the intelligence of the British Government of 1814-15.

With the treaty agreed to, the English Government became anxious about its ratification by President Madison. Significant evidence of this is furnished by Doctor Updyke, in his work from which we have already made a number of quotations. On page 355, Updyke says, "The British ministry had hoped that their last communication would enable the commissioners to close the negotiations for the treaty of peace. They were, however, suspicious of President Madison, and feared he would not sign the treaty. For this reason it was stipulated that the war should not cease until after the exchange of ratifications at Washington. They counted upon having a strong English fleet in the Chesapeake and the Delaware at the time that Baker, the bearer of the British copy of the treaty, should reach Washington; and they also counted upon the disposition of the Eastern states to secede from the Union, as likely to 'frighten Madison.' It was suggested that if Madison should refuse to ratify the treaty the British Government should immediately propose to make a separate treaty with the New England States, which it was believed could be accomplished."

Dr. Updyke gives as authority for the foregoing paragraph: "Liverpool to Castlereagh, December 23, 1814; Wellington Supplementary Dispatches, IX, 495."

Lord Liverpool was prime minister and Lord Castlereagh was secretary for foreign affairs.

The digest given of correspondence between these high English Government officials makes it plain that the English Government was anxious for ratification of the Peace Treaty and that they were fearful that Madison would not sign.

As confirmatory of the Liverpool apprehension it may be mentioned that the *London Times*, December 31, 1814 (see British Museum), said that the ratification by Madison depended upon the outcome of the expedition against New Orleans. The *London Times* was unfriendly to the Liverpool government, and was also very hostile to the United States. In the circumstances it may fairly be presumed that to allay criticism of the treaty the press was informed of the expected New Orleans coup.

In view of the unanimous action of the American Commissioners in agreeing to the Treaty, it becomes very evident that the British Government anticipated that something would transpire before the Treaty reached Washington that might cause the President to withhold his approval. In the light of present knowledge, that something was the expected British capture of New Orleans. We may well ask the question, as to why the British Government was so anxious for the ratification of the Treaty as to plan to "frighten Madison" and threaten separate peace with New England, thus disrupting the Union, if that Government expected to turn back Louisiana after its anticipated conquest. That question carries its own obvious answer.

Happily for us, and for England as consequences have proved, and for the world, the dilemma in which the English statesmen thought President Madison would be placed, was averted.

While Carroll, with the American copy of the Treaty, and Baker, with the English copy, also having authority to exchange ratification, ploughed the seas, an event was in the making of destiny, which, when brought forth, utterly confounded the carefully laid plans of the Liverpool-Castlereagh Government, and in fact ushered in a new epoch, a new and greater era for the young American Republic—never again to be pointed to as an experiment.

CHAPTER IX.

WASHINGTON, THE FIRST OF 1815.

One of the most thrilling incidents in our history is the reception by the country of the news of the Battle of New Orleans. It was theatrically acclaimed, with almost delirious joy, sharply contrasting with the condition of deep discouragement and gloom it suddenly dissipated. Seldom has a victory had more dramatic setting. It is well for us who enjoy the rich blessings of the present, occasionally to read of the trials and tribulations through which our forebears struggled, that they might hand these blessings down to us. "If an old man of perfect memory," says James Parton, in Chapter 20 of the second volume of the Life of Andrew Jackson, published in 1860, "were asked to name the time when the prospects of this republic were shrouded in deepest gloom, and the largest number of the people despaired of its future, his answer, I think, would be, 'the first thirty-seven days of the year 1815.'" (Parton makes an error of two days, for the news of the battle of New Orleans reached Washington February 4th.)

"The Capital," says Parton, "was in ruins" (as a result of its burning by the British the preceding August).

Parton further referred to the Hartford Convention, which on January 5th had closed several weeks of session. This anti-war convention was denounced as treasonable by administrative papers. It had aroused gravest apprehensions of disunion unless peace should at once be made.

In order to convey an idea of the antagonistic spirit prevailing, quotation is here given from the *Boston Gazette*, of that period: "Is there a Federalist, a patriot in America, who conceives it his duty to shed his blood for Bonaparte, for Madison and Jefferson, and that host of ruffians in Congress, who have set their faces against us for years, and spirited up the brutal part of the populace to destroy us? Not one! Shall we, then, any longer be held in slavery, and driven to desperate poverty by such a graceless faction?"

Parton further quotes many New England editors as saying: "No more taxes from New England, till the administration makes peace."

Parton further says that the great British expedition, so long mustering in the West Indies, so long delayed, cast a prodigious shadow before it, putting New York, Philadelphia and Baltimore on their guard; but that as the autumn passed without the reappearance of hostile force in the northern waters, the conviction gained ground that something overwhelming was in contemplation against the defenseless south and southwest.

"It so chanced," continues Parton, "that the 8th of January was the days on which it was first whispered about Washington that the President had received news of the British fleet at the mouth of the Mississippi. From that time the eyes of the country were fixed upon New Orleans—not hopefully."

"It is not an overstatement of the case," continues Parton, "to say that there was not one well informed man in the northern states who believed that New Orleans could be successfully defended."

Again quoting from Parton: "After a week of gossip and foreboding, came news of the gunboat battle, and its disastrous results; also rumors of a great armament hovering on the Atlantic coast. 'We are a lost country,' said the Federal papers in doleful concert. 'A wicked administration has ruined us. New Orleans having fallen an easy prey, the British General will leave a few acclimated black regiments to garrison that city, and bring the Wellington heroes around to the Chesapeake. Baltimore will not be able to resist. Washington will again be overrun, Philadelphia and New York will next be attacked, and who shall say with what results? See to what a pass Jefferson and French democracy have brought a deluded country!'"

All sorts of dire rumors were in circulation, and to add to the gloom that prevailed in Washington and elsewhere, a snow storm of remarkable violence and extent set in on the 23rd of January, and continued for three days. Belated mails straggled in, showing that the American Army was still resisting. "New Orleans is not taken yet," said the Western members, and the Republican editors. "It is merely a question of time," replied the Federalists; "the next mail will finish New Orleans and you."

In the midst of that setting, on February 4th, a horseman came into Washington, bearing glorious news for the Administration forces. He had dispatches from General Jackson, detailing the decisive victory of January 8th.

Washington was wild with delight at the unexpected victory. "That evening," still quoting from Parton, "the town was blazing with light, and the whole populace was abroad, now thronging about the White House (temporary), cheering the President, then surging around the houses of the Secretaries, and residences of the leading supporters of the war, rending the air with shouts.... The next issue of the *National Intelligencer* cannot be glanced over to this day without exciting in the mind something of the feeling which is wont to express itself by three times three and one cheer more. The great news was headed, in the *Intelligencer's* largest type, 'Almost Incredible Victory!!!!'"

It was worth a life time to experience the jubilation of that night! It was the sudden restoration of a people's national self-respect.

The news of the reception of the victory elsewhere was equally as thrilling. It aroused what Parton called the "maddest enthusiasm." A quotation may be given from the autobiography of Mr. John Binns: "A general illumination was ordered in Philadelphia. Few indeed there were yet there were a few who on that night closed their window shutters and mourned the defeat of the enemies of their country. I had early intelligence of this joyful news, and gladly, by an extra, spread it abroad.

I put scene painters to work, and had a transparency painted, which covered near-ly the whole front of my house. There had been a heavy snow fall, and there was that evening from nine to twelve inches of snow on the ground. That, however, did not prevent men, women and children from parading the street, and delighting their eyes by looking at the illumination and illuminated transparencies, which made the principal streets of our city as light as day. My transparency represented General Jackson on horseback at the head of his staff, in pursuit of the enemy, with the motto: 'This day shall ne'er go by, from this day to the ending of the world, but He, in it, shall be remembered.'"

This gives in brief a glimpse of the effect in the country of the news of the vic-tory at New Orleans. How can any American describe it as a needless battle? After the event it might have been deplored by the British as needless, just as any lost battle may be so regarded.

Just ten days after that lone horseman rode into Washington on February 4th, the Treaty reached the Capitol, and under the inspiration of the great victory at New Orleans, it was joyfully and speedily ratified.

CHAPTER X.

BUT WHAT IF THE ISSUE OF THE BATTLE HAD BEEN DIFFERENT?

As stated in the last chapter, the Peace Treaty was speedily and joyfully ratified. But what if the issue of the battle had been different?

The chronology of the Treaty may here be given:

Signed at Ghent, on the 24th day of December, 1814, by the Peace Commissioners representing the two countries;

Ratified for England by the Prince Regent on December 31st, 1814.

Reached Washington the night of February 14th, 1815;

Sent by President Madison to the Senate February 15th;

Ratification advised by the Senate, February 16th;

Ratified by President Madison February 17th, and ratification exchanged with England's representative the same day;

Promulgated by President Madison February 18th; thus ending the period of hostilities.

Would the United States Senate have advised ratification, or would the President have ratified, if the British on January 8th, had swept aside that defensive army and had carried into effect the design to capture and occupy Louisiana?

Probably no more grave or serious situation has ever confronted an American President than that which would have been presented. By ratifying the treaty, the President would have satisfied the New England malcontents, who had given veiled threats of disunion. But by the ratification with England in possession of Louisiana, and holding that it was not a legal possession of the United States, the President would have faced a desperate alternative of giving up Louisiana, and the trans-Mississippi territory; or referring it to the issue of a future war, or future negotiations.

It is the belief of the writer that President Madison would have declined to ratify the Treaty, as long as the British remained in occupation of Louisiana; thus prolonging the war with its uncertainties, and taking the risk of the disruption of the Union, through a separate peace with England by the New England States; a proposition which, as we have seen, was in contemplation by the English Government.

All of these questions, so momentous, to the American Union, were happily and gloriously averted by the marvelous defensive victory at New Orleans.

And yet, American historians teach our children that that battle was a needless one!

Oh, ignorance! Oh, prejudice! Oh, pro-English!!

CHAPTER XI.

TESTIMONY FROM GENERAL JACKSON HIM-SELF.

In presenting this case against the school historians, which he feels has already been made, to the satisfaction of any impartial reader, the writer has refrained from using much confirmatory material in order to be as brief as possible. But in the history of Andrew Jackson, written by A. C. Buell, and published in 1904, there occurs illuminating data highly apropos in this connection. It may be remarked that Buell is not a favorite of some historians. Buell was distinctly not pro-English.

In chapter 3 of the second volume of Buell's history, entitled "British Designs on Louisiana," the author reiterates a statement before made, that Jackson's Army of New Orleans saved the Louisiana Purchase, and adds that few people of the millions who were celebrating in 1904 the centenary of the colossal transaction between Napoleon Bonaparte and Thomas Jefferson, realized the significance of these words. Buell later says: "Viewed in the light of its actual influence on the map of North America, and the fortunes of this Republic, it was the most import-ant battle ever fought between Great Britain and the United States.... The real, vast, enduring value of the Battle of New Orleans, lay in the fact that it prevented an-other war."

In adducing evidence of the purpose of the English Government against Lou-isiana, Buell says: "The fleet carried more than an army, the narratives of the sub-altern and Capt. Cooke, reputable British officers of 85th and 43rd Light Infantry, respectively, tell us there was on board the fleet 'a complete civil government staff' to be installed in place of the State Government of Louisiana at the moment of oc-cupation. One of them, with a spice of humor, informs us that one member of this 'civil government staff' was 'a worthy Colonial official whose confidence in the success of the Expedition led him to resign the comfortable position of Collector of Barbadoes to take the larger and more lucrative post for the (to-be) Crown Colony of Louisiana."

As other members of the civil government staff Mr. Buell names Honorable Mr. Elwood, Lieut. Governor, transferred from Trinidad, and Mr. Dockstader, transferred from upper Canada; also an Attorney-General, an Admiralty Judge, and a Secretary of the Colony, sent from England direct.

Mr. Buell continues: "Besides his general orders at Plymouth, Pakenham brought with him a proclamation approved by the Home Government or Colonial office. This proclamation was to be published as soon as the British Army should occupy New Orleans. It promised protection to everybody, general amnesty to all previously engaged in hostilities, and proclaimed the sovereignty of England, in behalf of Spain, over all the territory fraudulently conveyed by Bonaparte to the United States. It denied the validity of the secret treaty by which Spain re-ceded Louisiana to France in 1800. It denied Bonaparte's right to act for France in 1803. And finally it 'denounced the pretentions of the United States to sovereignty under the alleged purchase from Bonaparte.' This proclamation was in printed form at British headquarters the night before the battle, and its contents were well known to many British officers. The night after the battle it disappeared. Every copy of it was burned!

"All this evidence was obtained from British prisoners taken in the battle of January 8th. But it lacked one link to make the chain perfect. That was evidence of specific design and fixed policy on the part of the British Government. In the absence of such evidence the cabinet of St. James might, in emergency, declare that the scheme of a 'crown colony' and the proclamation itself were the acts of General Pakenham—to be approved if he succeeded or disavowed if he failed. The needed link was supplied long after."

"The final link in the chain," says Mr. Buell, "was furnished by General Jackson himself. In the fall of 1875, the author, then a staff correspondent of the *Missouri Republican*, visited former Governor William Allen, of Ohio, at his farm near Chillicothe. During the visit, which was of three days' duration, the venerable statesman's conversation—when not upon agricultural subjects—was mainly of reminiscences of his earlier public life. All was interesting; some of it historically valuable, particularly those parts relating to the British invasion of Louisiana. What Governor Allen said on this subject we reproduce here, exactly as it was printed in 1875."

Governor Allen's interview is here given in full:

"Near the end of General Jackson's second administration and shortly after the admission of Arkansas to the Union, I, being Senator elect from Ohio, went to Washington to take the seat on March 4th.

"General Jackson,—he always preferred to be called General rather than Mr. President, and so we always addressed him by his military title—General Jackson invited me to lunch with him. No sooner were we seated than he said: 'Mr. Allen, let us take a little drink to the new star in the flag—Arkansas.' This ceremony being duly observed, the General said: 'Allen, if there had been disaster instead of victory at New Orleans, there never would have been a state of Arkansas.'"

"This, of course, interested me, and I asked: 'Why do you say that, General?'

"Then he said, that if Pakenham had taken New Orleans, the British would have claimed and held the whole Louisiana Purchase. But I said: 'You know, General Jackson, that the treaty of Ghent, which had been signed fifteen days before the battle, provided for restoration of all territory, places and possessions taken by either nation from the other during the war, with certain unimportant exceptions.'

"'Yes, of course,' he replied, 'But the minutes of the conference at Ghent as kept by Mr. Gallatin, represent the British commissioners as declaring in exact words: 'We do not admit Bonaparte's construction of the law of nations; and we cannot accept it in relation to any subject matter before us.'

"'At that moment,' pursued General Jackson, 'none of our Commissioners knew what the real meaning of these words was. When they were uttered, the British Commissioners knew that Pakenham's expedition had been decided on. Our Commissioners did not know it. Now, since I have been Chief Magistrate, I have learned from diplomatic sources of the most unquestionable authority, that the British ministry did not intend the Treaty of Ghent to apply to the Louisiana Purchase at all. The whole corporation of them, from 1803 to 1815—Pitt, the Duke of Portland, Granville, Percival, Lord Liverpool and Castlereagh—denied the legal right of Napoleon to sell Louisiana to us, and they held, therefore, that we had no right to that territory. So you see, Allen, that the words of Mr. Goulburn, on behalf of the British Commissioners, which I have quoted to you from Albert Gallatin's Minutes of the Conference, had a far deeper significance than our commissioners could perpetrate. Those words were meant to lay the foundation for a claim on the Louisiana Purchase entirely external to the provisions of the Treaty of Ghent. And in that way the British Government was signing a treaty with one hand in front while with the other hand behind its back it was despatching Pakenham's army to seize the fairest of our possessions.

"'You can also see, my dear William,' said the old General, waxing warm (having once or twice more during the luncheon toasted the new star), 'you can also see what an awful mess such a situation would have been if the British programme had been carried out in full. But Providence willed otherwise. All the tangled web that the cunning of the English Diplomats could weave around our unsuspecting commissioners at Ghent was torn to pieces and soaked with British blood in half an hour at New Orleans by the never-missing rifles of my Tennessee and Kentucky pioneers. And that ended it. British diplomacy could do wonders, but it couldn't provide against such a contingency as that. The British Commissioners could throw sand in the eyes of ours at Ghent, but they couldn't help the cold lead that my riflemen sprinkled in the faces of their soldiers at New Orleans. Now, Allen, you have the whole story. Now you know why Arkansas was saved at New Orleans. Let's take another little one.'"

Thomas E. Watson, at one time United States Senator from Georgia, in a history of Jackson, written after Buell's history, quotes this interview and comments that it settles the question, and that if the British had captured New Orleans, the United States boundary line would have stopped at the Mississippi.

CHAPTER XII.

CAPTAIN GARLAND'S TESTIMONY ON THE SPOT.

Captain Henry Garland was one of Jackson's young officers at New Orleans. In view of the brilliance and stirring eloquence of a speech made by him, which I am about to give, from the same chapter heretofore quoted from Buell, it will be interesting to give a digest of Buell's description of him: He was born at Nantes, France, his father a merchant of Norfolk, Virginia, residing there as Commercial Agent for American importing houses. He received his education in French schools. Coming to America, he went to Tennessee, and in the War of 1812 volunteered in Coffee's mounted riflemen, serving with distinction throughout the war.

In the latter part of March, 1815, the officers of the Louisiana militia gave a banquet to those of the Tennessee, Kentucky and Mississippi troops and the Regulars, on the eve of the disbandment of Jackson's Army. Captain Garland was selected by his comrades to respond in French on their behalf.

"The guests," said Buell, "were welcomed on behalf of the Creole hosts and hostesses by Vicar-General, the Most Reverend Abbe Dubourg, Bishop of Louisiana, who made a brief address of welcome, first in English and then in French. In conclusion, the Abbe expressed sorrow that such an awful battle should have been fought and so many souls sent unprepared into the presence of the Creator, two weeks after the Treaty of Peace had been signed on the other side of the Ocean."

According to Buell, the Abbe's remarks changed the whole character of Garland's reply. He spoke in French, which was afterwards translated.

The writer recommends a full reading of this, at points, remarkably eloquent speech, from which some excerpts are here given.

After some introductory remarks, Captain Garland said: "The most reverend prelate, in his otherwise well chosen remarks, suggested that it was a pity that such an awful battle should have been fought after the Treaty was signed across the wide water. I do not agree with him. It needed that battle to make the Treaty good. It made no difference when the Treaty was signed. Without that battle it must have been waste paper.

"The Treaty as written, did not mean anything. It says that the territorial status quo ante bellum shall be observed. But the British Cabinet held 'l'arriere pensee' about that. They never admitted Napoleon's right to convey Louisiana to us through President Jefferson. They did not mean to include the Louisiana Purchase in the territorial status quo ante bellum!

"The Treaty signed in ink on the 24th of December was a cheat. But the Treaty that the Pioneers of Tennessee and Kentucky punctuated with rifle bullets the 8th of January will stand. The English diplomats at Ghent held, as I have said, 'l'arriere-pensee.' But the British soldiers who lay down to die in front of Kentucky and Tennessee the 8th of January on Chalmette plain were sincere and honest. It was in their life blood that the real treaty was written; not in the ink of Ghent.

"The English plan of subjugation was complete. Soon after the battle it was learned that General Pakenham had a proclamation written, signed and ready to be promulgated the moment his Army should enter the City. This proclamation denied the right of Napoleon to sell Louisiana, denounced the pretentions of the United States to its sovereignty, declared that Spain, the rightful possessor, was incapable of maintaining her territorial rights, and, finally, asserted a provisional occupation by the British forces as a virtual protectorate in behalf of the Spanish Crown. The night after the battle, this proclamation was burned. It may have been used to illuminate the scene where the corpse of its author was being prepared for shipment to England in a cask of rum.

"It is commonly known that, the night of January 7th, a council of war was held in the British camp. It is also known to many that, on that occasion, Major-General Sir Samuel Gibbs spoke of General Jackson's Army as a 'backwoods rabble.' He was right. That's what we are—from the point of view of a British regular. We are 'Backwoodsmen,' because we were born and raised in little log cabins all along our great frontier. The mothers who gave us milk, made their own clothes, and ours, too, of homespun or of buckskin. As soon as we could lift a rifle we had to hunt our meat in the woods. Yes, we are 'backwoodsmen.' And from the point of view of a British regular, we are a 'rabble,' too. That is, we are not soldiers in the regular sense of the term. We are not enlisted; we don't get any pay. We are simply assembled, as volunteers, to defend our country. We have a kind of organization, it is true; but it is as independent companies, composed of neighbors, and our officers are simply those men whose characters and experience point them out as natural leaders. In one word, we have no regulations, except those of common sense; no discipline, except that of common consent; no mastery, one over the other, except that of manhood! Such are the men who rallied from Tennessee and Kentucky when Andrew Jackson called.

"Yes, Ladies and Gentlemen, they are a 'backwoods rabble.' They met, say, three times their number of soldiers who were the Pride of England! And the 'Backwoods Rabble' laid that 'Pride of England' low!"

* * * * * * * *

"And now just one word more: Most people say that our American Republic was born the fourth day of July, 1776, at Philadelphia. This is not true. It was only begotten then. It was born when Burgoyne surrendered at Saratoga. It was baptised when Cornwallis yielded at Yorktown. But it was never confirmed, as they say in the religion of the Holy Saviour, until the 8th of last January!

"That day saw not merely the repulse and destruction of a British Army, but it taught the whole world a lesson never to be forgot. It needs not the gift of prophecy to foresee that the battle fought by Andrew Jackson and his 'backwoods rabble' did more than repulse cowardly and treacherous invasion. It taught to all the princes and kings and emperors on the face of the earth that they must let our young Republic alone!"

Apart from his testimony as to Pakenham's intended proclamation, and apart from his estimate of British diplomacy, the speech of Captain Garland is well worth preserving as a specimen of real, patriotic eloquence.

* * * * * * * *

From the mass of evidence, available to any earnest historian, the writer has selected one more witness, whose testimony is compressed, in an incidental paragraph. At the meeting of the American Historical Association in New Orleans in 1903, Dr. W. M. Sloane read a paper entitled, "The World Aspects of the Louisiana Purchase." It is published in Volume I of the "Proceedings of the American Historical Association of 1903." In that paper (page 102 of Proceedings above cited) appears this sentence: "But for Jefferson's wisdom in explorating it (Louisiana) might have remained a wilderness long after settlement began; Great Britain coveted it in 1815 when Jackson saved it." There is a sentence compact with fact. Dr. William M. Sloane (now dead) was at the time of the address, and for many years professor of history at Princeton University, and a recognized authority on history.

In all literature there cannot be found a more concrete, comprehensive line: "Great Britain coveted it in 1815 when Jackson saved it." Pro-English historians may deftly turn and twist this and other facts to their purpose; but let me give a tocsin call: PRO-ENGLISH HISTORIANS SHOULD BE KEPT OUT OF OUR SCHOOLS, AND YOUNG AMERICA TAUGHT ONLY THE UNGARBLED, UNVARNISHED TRUTH.

CHAPTER XIII.

RECAPITULATION.

The writer, in these pages, has shown by what must be conceded on all sides, irrefragable evidence that school histories are in error in saying the Battle of New Orleans was fought after peace, and was therefore a needless battle.

The writer has also shown by evidence he considers conclusive, that England held as invalid the title of the United States to Louisiana, acquired by sale from Bonaparte to the United States in 1803; that England deliberately planned the conquest of Louisiana (with the resultant development, if successful, of a great dominion to the west of the United States, like Canada on the North). That evidence is mainly furnished by the British themselves. First in the British note to the United States Peace Commissioners, criticizing the title of the United States to Louisiana; and, second, in the fitting out and dispatching of the expedition against New Orleans during the peace negotiations; in the complete Civil Government staff, for Louisiana, carried by the expedition; in the record of the peace negotiations, first in the insistence by the British upon the Uti Possidetis principle, and, second, when that failed, in the proposal of words to be inserted in the Mutual Restoration clause, which proposal finally resulted in the word, "Possessions" in that clause, under which England could hold that Louisiana, having been taken, was not subject to return, not being a possession of the United States; further in the letter of Prime Minister Liverpool to Lord Castlereagh, assuming British occupation of New Orleans, outlining purpose to "frighten Madison" into signing the Treaty (thus leaving England in possession of Louisiana).

After close and careful study, the writer presents as a summary of his conclusion as to the value of the Battle of New Orleans:

First, that it was a highly necessary battle on the part of the United States, rendered so by British aggression;

Second, that the statement in school and other histories that it was fought after peace is entirely false, the Peace Treaty itself being evidence. (All historians, past, present, and to come, cannot change the text of that Treaty);

Third, that it saved the Louisiana Purchase to the United States or averted another war with England;

Fourth, that it settled forever the question of the title to Louisiana;

Fifth, that it created a profound impression on the world. Speaking, as one orator has put it, in language all nations could understand, that the young American

Republic had the will to be free and the power to enforce that will;

Sixth, that it marked the last time that the foot of a foreign foe has been set on American soil, except when Mexico invaded Texas in 1846;

Seventh, that it practically added to the Peace Treaty that impressment and orders in council would no longer be imposed by England, for these obnoxious policies were never sought to be revived;

Eighth, that it saved this sorely harassed, nearly treason-torn country, at a critical time in its life, from threatened and possible disunion, and re-established national self-respect;

Ninth, that it made Andrew Jackson a national hero, resulting in his election as President of the United States, and the establishment of what is known as the Jackson era;

Tenth, that it resulted in mutual respect and friendship between the United States and England, which has endured to this day, and which it is hoped will perpetually endure.

Could any battle have had a greater or more varied effect?

School historians and other historians, in appraising the battle as a needless and useless one, do violence to truth and grossly impose upon Young America, as well as America in general.

The underlying American sentiment of honor, truth and justice demands revision of these school histories, and that right speedily.

In conclusion, the writer recommends, as revision, in those histories which desire to dispose of the Battle of New Orleans in a paragraph, the following:

The Battle of New Orleans, fought January 8, 1815, was one of the most brilliant defensive victories in history. Many historians have classed it as a needless victory in that it was fought after peace. That is an error, for the Peace Treaty, signed by the Commissioners of the two countries, December 24, 1814, specifically provided that it should not be effective until ratified by both sides. It was not ratified by the United States until February 17, 1815, soon after its reception. The news of the victory came at a critical time in the history of the country, and was received with great enthusiasm everywhere. It settled forever all question as to the title of the United States to Louisiana. It saved Louisiana, or a least averted another war with England. It resulted in lasting, solid peace with England, which should permanently endure. As illustration of the character of that peace, it may be pointed out that the boundary line between the United States and Canada extending about three thousand miles, has not, on either side, a fort or fortification. God help the English-speaking people if one should ever be necessary!

THE END.

ADDENDA.

WORDING OF THE TREATY OF GHENT.

In addition to the references cited on pages 7 and 21 as to the full text of the Treaty of Ghent reference may be given to volume compiled by Hunter Miller entitled: "Treaties and Other International Acts of the United States of America." (See volume 2, pages 574-584.)

ENGLISH CRITICISM OF U. S. TITLE TO LOUISIANA.

The third and fourth paragraphs of the note of the British Commissioners to the American Commissioners at Ghent October 8, 1814, read as follows:

In adverting for this purpose to the acquisition of Louisiana, the undersigned must observe that the instrument by which the consent of His Catholic Majesty is alleged to have been given to the cession of it has never been made public. His Catholic Majesty was no party to the treaty by which the cession was made, and if any sanction has been subsequently obtained from him, it must have been, like other contemporaneous acts of that monarch, involuntary, and, as such, cannot alter the character of the transaction. The Marquis of Yrujo, the minister of His Catholic Majesty at Washington, in a letter addressed to the President of the United States, formally protested against the cession, and the right of France to make it; yet in the face of this protestation, so strongly evincing the decided opinion of Spain as to the illegality of the proceeding, the President of the United States ratified the treaty. Can it be contended that the annexation of Louisiana, under such circumstances, did not mark a spirit of territorial aggrandizement?

His Britannic Majesty did certainly express satisfaction when the American Government communicated the event that Louisiana, a valuable colony in the possession of France, with whom the war had just been renewed, instead of remaining in the hands of his enemy, had been ceded to the United States, at that time professing the most friendly disposition towards Great Britain, and an intention of providing for her interest in the acquisition. But the conditions under which France had acquired Louisiana from Spain were not communicated; the refusal of Spain to consent to its alienation was not known; the protest of her ambassador had not been made; and many other circumstances attending the transaction, on which it is now unnecessary to dilate, were, as there is good to believe, industriously concealed. (From American State Papers, Foreign Relations, Volume III, page 721.)

The reply of the American Commissioners is quoted on page 26 of this volume.

(Author's note: From the foregoing we can better understand the refusal of the British Commissioners to discuss the northern boundary of Louisiana as proposed in American note of November 10. See page 26, this volume.)

THE UTI POSSIDETIS PROPOSAL.

The note of the British Commissioners, October 21, 1814, contained the following paragraph:

In regard to other boundaries, the American plenipotentiaries, in their note of August 24, appeared in some measure to object to the propositions then made by the undersigned, as not being on the basis of uti possidetis. The undersigned are willing to treat on that basis, subject to such modifications as mutual convenience may be found to require; and they trust that the American plenipotentiaries will show, by their ready acceptance of this basis, that they duly appreciate the moderation of His Majesty's Government in so far consulting the honor and fair pretensions of the United States as, in the relative situation of the two countries, to authorize such a proposition. (From American State Papers, Foreign Relations, Volume III.)

(Author's note: This is an adroit effort to put upon the Americans the initial suggestion of the Uti Possidetis. The Americans, after seeing the futility of any treaty agreement as to impressment and trade restriction, adhered steadily to the Status Quo Ante Bellum basis. They rejected the Uti Possidetis principle. It should be borne in mind that at the time of the above note the secret expedition against Louisiana, assembling in Nigril Bay, Jamaica, was nearing completion.)

TIME OF EFFECTIVENESS OF TREATY.

On November 10, 1814, the American Commissioners submitted a *projet* of a treaty containing in article one the statement that "All hostilities, both by sea and land, shall immediately cease," and in article fifteen the statement that "This treaty, when the same shall have been ratified on both sides, and the respective ratifications mutually exchanged, shall be binding upon both parties, and the ratifications shall be exchanged at _______ in the space of _______ months from this day, or sooner if possible."

On November 26 the British Commissioners returned the *projet*, altered to read that "All hostilities, both by sea and land, shall cease after the exchange of ratifications as hereafter mentioned," and that "This treaty, when the same shall have ratified on both sides, and the ratifications mutually exchanged, shall be binding on both parties, and the ratifications shall be exchanged at Washington with all practical despatch, in the space of _______ months from this day, or sooner if practicable."

On November 30, 1814, the American Commissioners stated in a note to the British Commissioners:

The undersigned consent that the day of the exchange of the ratifications be substituted to that of the signature of the treaty as the time for the cessation of hostilities, and for regulating the periods after which prizes at sea shall be restored; it being understood that measures shall be adopted for a speedy exchange of ratifications. (American State Papers, Foreign Relations, Volume III.)

(Author's note: It will thus be seen that the British proposed the date of ratification as the time of the effectiveness of the treaty, and the cessation of hostilities, and that the Americans consented, thus carrying into the treaty the provision so uniformly overlooked by our historians.)

PASSAMAQUODDY ISLANDS.

(Author's note: There was towards the end of the negotiations at Ghent much and voluminous correspondence, mainly on the part of the British, concerning the question involved in the Passamaquoddy Islands situation; it was magnified, admittedly, out of proportion to the subject involved, especially in view of the fact that the final disposition of these fisheries was relegated to a civil commission to meet after peace. The British, while conceding the relative insignificance of the islands, maintained that a question of honor was involved which might "prove an insuperable bar to the conclusion of peace at the present time." In reading the mass of British correspondence on the subject of these islands one is forced to the conclusion that there was an underlying purpose.)

AS TO WORDING IN MUTUAL RESTORATION CLAUSE.

The American *projet* of November 10 contained also the proposition that all territory, places, and possessions "taken by either party from the other during the war, or which may be taken after the signing of this treaty, shall be restored."

The *projet* returned on November 26 by the British Commissioners was altered to read all territory, places, and possessions, "belonging to either party and taken by the other during the war, or which may be taken after the signing of this treaty, shall be restored."

The protocol of a conference of the American and British Commissioners, held on December 1, contained the following statements:

At a conference held this day, the American plenipotentiaries proposed the following alterations in their *projet*, as amended by the British plenipotentiaries: 1st—In article I, strike out the alteration consisting of the words "belonging to," and "taken by," and preserve the original reading, viz: "taken by either party from the other."

This alteration was objected to by the British plenipotentiaries, and, after some discussion, reserved by them for the consideration of their Government. (Ibid., pages 735, 742.)

(Author's note: The American Commissioners stated in a note December 14, to the British Commissioners that they agreed to accept the British proposal to "omit the words originally offered by them," provided that the Passamaquoddy Islands should alone be excepted from the mutual restoration of territory. See American State Papers, Volume III, pages 743, 744, for full text of note. Also for text of letter from British Commissioners to British Government as of December 13, see Photostat in Library of Congress from Public Record Office, London—Foreign Office 5, Vol. 102. Thus in the mutual restoration clause of the treaty the words "all places, points, and 'possessions' whatsoever," went in, without the clarifying term as to "possessions" proposed by the British. Did the British Government deem the clarification essential? Evidence, too strong for disbelief, shows it did not. The secret expedition against Louisiana was then well on its way, and expected to be in possession of New Orleans any day, with the full set of civil officers, carried on Admiral Cochran's fleet, installed and in control. Evidence has been given showing the anxiety of British officials, after the signing of the treaty, as to its ratification by President Madison. If the British plans against Louisiana had succeeded would President Madison have ratified the treaty? That is a fair question for College debate.)

Lector House believes that a society develops through a two-fold approach of continuous learning and adaptation, which is derived from the study of classic literary works spread across the historic timeline of literature records. Therefore, we aim at reviving, repairing and redeveloping all those inaccessible or damaged but historically as well as culturally important literature across subjects so that the future generations may have an opportunity to study and learn from past works to embark upon a journey of creating a better future.

This book is a result of an effort made by Lector House towards making a contribution to the preservation and repair of original ancient works which might hold historical significance to the approach of continuous learning across subjects.

HAPPY READING & LEARNING!

LECTOR HOUSE LLP
E-MAIL: lectorpublishing@gmail.com